GLASGOW
THE PEOPLE'S STORY

1. August 1945 sees these Glasgow youngsters building a victory blaze.

2. Dancing in the park at Kelvingrove, August 1945

GLASGOW
THE PEOPLE'S STORY

Fifty Years of
Photographs 1945 - 95

Editor
Paul Harris

A Paul Harris book for

LOMOND BOOKS

in association with

THE GLASWEGIAN

A Paul Harris book for Lomond Books Ltd

Text and arrangement © copyright Paul Harris 1996
All photographs © copyright The Scottish Daily Record & Sunday Mail Ltd 1996
excepting photograph no. 218 © copyright Stephen Gibson
ISBN 0 9514985 1 7

First published 1996 by
Lomond Books Ltd
36 West Shore Road
Granton
Edinburgh EH5 1QD

in association with

The Glaswegian
Anderston Quay
Glasgow G3 8DA

Other Paul Harris books published by Lomond
Glasgow Since 1900
Edinburgh Since 1900
Edinburgh: The Fabulous Fifties
Aberdeen Since 1900
Aberdeen at War

All the photographs in this book are from the library at The Scottish Daily Record &
Sunday Mail Ltd. Any enquiries regarding these pictures - either for reproduction rights
or for copies/prints - should be made to The Library Manager at The Picture Library,
Scottish Daily Record & Sunday Mail Ltd., Anderston Quay, Glasgow G3 8DA.
Telephone 0141-242-3523.

Production by Paul Harris
Whittingehame House
Haddington EH41 4QA

Printed by Gorenjski tisk Printing Company, Kranj
Republic of Slovenia

CONTENTS

ACKNOWLEDGEMENTS

This book is a follow up to *Glasgow Since 1900* which has now gone through three separate printings since it first appeared in 1989. I would like to think that the success of the book is a reflection of the increased confidence and optimism of the Glaswegian over the last decade. Certainly, the changes of the last fifty years would have seemed barely credible just over fifty years ago as the soldiers came home from the war and danced in the streets of a city still largley reliant on Victorian industry and Victorian values increasingly inappropriate in the modern world. As we approach the end of the millenium it seems a good time to look back over the last fifty years in Glasgow.
The results are, I think, encouraging.

My thanks go to everyone at the Picture Library of the Scottish Daily Record and Sunday Mail who helped me in researching and looking out the phtographs for this book. Especial thanks go to Mrs Pat Baird and Colin MacMillan, and to Euan Cameron, Paul O'Donnel and Timmy Galloway who scanned the images in record time.

This book is associated with *The Glaswegian* newspaper, part of the Scottish Daily Record & Sunday Mail Ltd. Although *The Glaswegian* was founded in 1989, the group as a whole enjoys a long history of 100 years. Much has changed in that period and although many of the pictures in this book may appear deeply nostalgic - if not downright quaint - the picture collection at the heart of the newspapers' Anderston Quay building is now a growing, state-of-the-art electronic information resource, where the latest technology has been harnessed to convert the existing picture library into a growing archive of electronic images.

Any mistakes are, of course, entirely my own and I am always grateful if they are pointed out to me !

Paul Harris
June 1996

CORD
SUNDAY MAIL
EVENING NEWS
KEMSLEY HOUSE
V
onal Newspapers

THE CHANGING FACE
OF THE CITY

4. This 1969 picture graphically demonstrates old and new existing side by side as a horse and cart passes beneath new high rise flats.

3. Glaswegians celebrating the end of war outside the Daily Record and Sunday Mail offices in Hope Street.

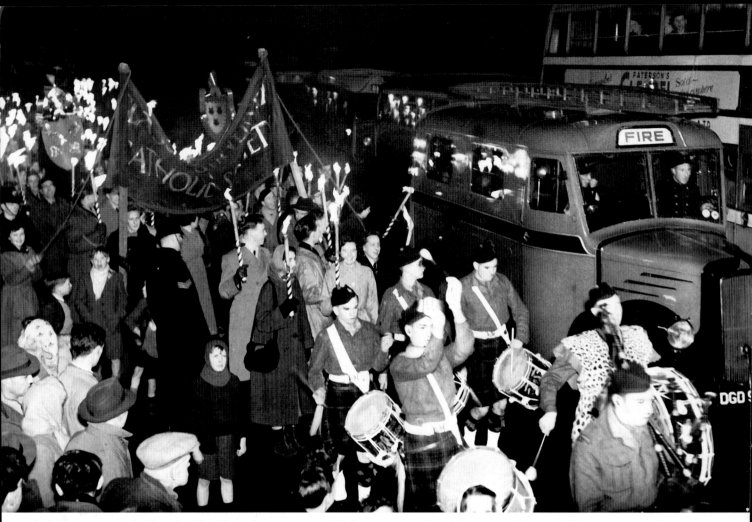

5. A fire engine is held up in John Knox Street by a torchlight procession in celebration of Glasgow University's 500th anniversary, January 1951.

6. There were relatively few vehicles on the road in the early 1950s and a road accident was a notable occurence. This accident was at the corner of Edmiston Drive and Copland Road, January 1952.

7. St. Vincent Street, 1949.

8. Demolition work high above Argyle Street in preparation for building a new Littlewoods store, 1950.

9. Street scene in St George's Cross outside the Wood Selby department store in the early 1950s.

10. Crossing the Clyde, 1955. Victoria Bridge, Stockwell Street, is uncluttered by traffic.

11. Crossing the Clyde, 1965. Ten years later and it is clear the motor car is taking over !

2. *Top left* The cry of "Coal !" was a familiar one to Gorbals residents.

3. Home grown adventure playground in the Gorbals, 1964.

4. Old and new together, Townhead. In 1970 there was controversy over the council's failure to demolish these abandoned tenements in the shadow of the proud new high rises. In time, people would become nostalgic about these tenement dwellings.

5. *Above* At first, new residents liked the amenity and comfort of their modern flats. This home, photographed in 1973, was on the seventh floor of a 1969 block on the Wyndford Estate in Maryhill. Tenant Mrs Vera Renor said she liked it very much - and thought it was excellent value at £19.50 a month, inclusive of rates !

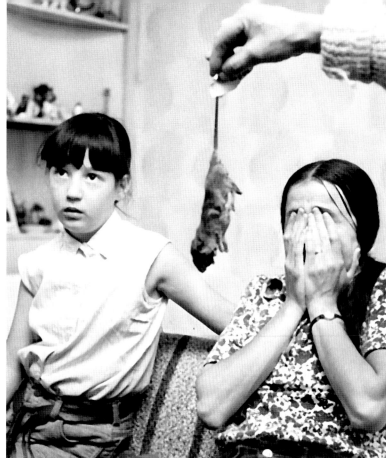

6. In this 1966 photograph high rise construction in the Gorbals seems to symbolise the hope for a better future.

7. *Above left* Not everybody was so keen to leave their tenement homes. Mrs Mary Sinclair was the last person to leave her block in Matheson Street. She liked to keep her budgie on the window sill . . .

8. There were some truly grim aspects to life in the Gorbals. John Williams, his wife and children lived in a Hospital Street tenement flat infested by rats. He told reporters they had been plagued by the rodents for five years.

9. *Opposite* The Red Road flats in Balornock were the highest tower blocks in Europe when they were built in the 1960s. Ten years later, they were dubbed The Dread Road Flats: eight concrete blocks, some as high as 31 storeys, crammed with 4,500 people.

0. *Opposite* The love affair with the modern blocks would eventually end. Here the Hutchesontown E complex, built in 1972, is demolished in June 1987 after having lain empty for six years - plagued by dampness, construction faults and brown asbestos.

1. This house in Milngavie was built in 1936 for £710, including the land it stood on. In the early 1970s it was worth £10,000 and the *Record* observed that 'colossal inflation' was hitting houses.

2. In 1956 this construction was regarded with some awe. It was the so-called 'Six Day House'. It is an All-Bellrock House at Switchback Road, Garscube, erected in just six days. The exterior walls - made of gypsum and honeycomb panelling - took just three hours to put up!

3. *Above* Many children missed the back courts of the old tenements where they could play in safety. In the early '70s these kids in Hutchesontown set out to build their own playground in Lawmoor Street.

24. The new shopping centre in St Enoch Square takes shape, December 1987. Its design was revolutionary and people wondered exactly what was being built . . .

25. Once completed, the St. Enoch Centre was dubbed by some "the largest greenhouse in Europe".

ALL NIGHT LONG . . .

26. Crowds outside the La Scala Cinema in Sauchiehall Street watch celebrtities arrive for the world premiere of a long forgotten film entitled *A Man Called Peter*, the story of a Coatbridge-born minister who became pastor to the American Senate.
March 31 1955.

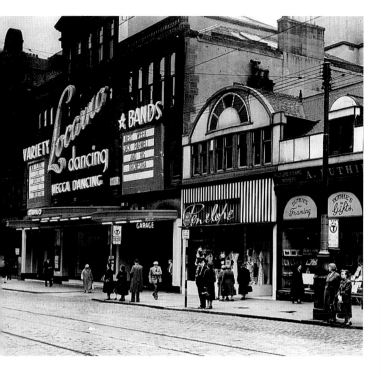

7. In the Barrowland Ballroom in January 1962, Catherine McLeod throws herself into the latest craze, The Twist.

8. The Locarno.

9. The Barrowland Ballroom, a legend in Glasgow nightlife.

30. Police officers arrive outside the Plaza Ballroom, Charing Cross, in the early 1970s.

31., 34. *Above and opposite* Rock and roll was all the craze in Glasgow's dance halls in the mid 1950s. Here these Glasgow enthusiasts demonstrate how it's done, led by team leaders Johnny Wilson and Betty Allan (opposite).

32. 1960s cha-cha from champions Andrew Cowan and Margaret Matheson at the Dennistoun Palais.

33. Grooving, man, 1970s style.

35. Manager Charles Lochrie watches operators checking the projector before the opening of Gasgow's News Cinema - the Classic - in Renfield Street in 1956.

36. By the early 70s old style cinemas were on the slide. Children protest in Rutherglen against the closure of The Odeon, 1972.

37. Past times. Cinema usherette Dorothy Smith took the cash at the front and popped up at the front of the auditorium in the intervals to sell Eldorado ice cream.

38. Cinema architecture was nothing if not exotic. The Vogue in Knightswood was part oriental, part modernist in design.

39. The 2,000 capacity New Bedford Cinema in Eglinton Street was erected in just 20 weeks and enjoyed spectacular floodlighting.

40. In the late1980s multi-screen cinemas started to arrive on out of town sites close to major shopping centres. The first to open in Scotland was the AMC, dubbed the 'Macdonalds of the cinema', which opened a 10 screen complex in Clydebank in 1988.

SPECIAL OFFER:
2 BOTTLES BEST WHISKY
1 BOTTLE FINE OLD PORT - 8'3

1 BOTTLE BEST WHISKY
1½ BOTTLE FINE OLD PORT - 4'2

41. *Left* No, this is not the broo but a queue for the brew. This 1965 picture recalls that pubs were not allowed to open on Sundays in Scotland and just before 6.30 p.m. opening time these Glaswegians are queuing outside a hotel bar waiting for sustenance.

42. In 1947 a nip of whisky in a Glasgow pub came in at 2s 7d - about 13 pence. The prices on the board - even cheaper - are 1905 prices.

43. But, in Parliamentary Road, this publican was selling nips at 1s a time in 1953 - a real bargain in those days.

44. The new cocktail bar of the Corn Exchange, Glasgow, October 1960.

5. The wide sweep of the Copacabana's mahogany bar, a favourite trendy resting place for Glaswegian elbows in the 1960s.

46. The Logan family - Pa, Ma, Jimmy and Bud - survey the damage to their dream, the Metropole Theatre, from the stage of the burned out theatre in 1961.

47. The Metropole burns.

48. The Alhambra Theatre demolished 1971. These workers doing a dance in the rubble seem to have no regrets. Left to right: Willie Barr, Robert Hollis, Tom Freeman, Alex McCartney, Neil McGlouchon, Dougie MacMillom, Angus Henderson and Eddie Livingston. Looking on from the box are Joe Byrne and William McMillom, bosses of the demolition firm.

49. Twisting the night away at the New Locarno in 1962 are a trio of 19-year-olds: Netta Whyte of Penilee, Maureen McGilvray of Hillington, and Sandra Stroyan of Penilee.

50. Art students gather at Central Station for their annual dance in 1967.

51. Drumchapel's New Generation Rock Team was made up of 16 youngsters from the Argo Youth Centre in 1977. Left to right: Elizabeth Clark, Jim Smith, Julie Fox, Janus Wards, Wendy Danks, David Clark.

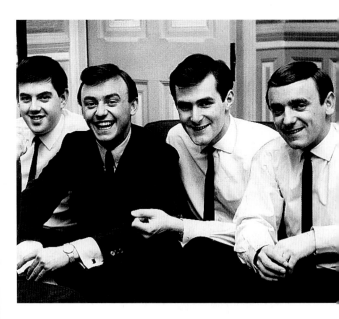

52. Kenny Ball at the Kelvin Hall in 1967, pictured with Miss Record, Catherine Cummings.

53. Gerry and the Pacemakers in Glasgow 1964.

54. Rod Stewart outside the City Chambers in 1976 with Drumchapel woman Louise McInnes. Not his latest girlfriend but a prizewinner in the Glasgow Students' Charities Appeal !

TRANSPORT EXPLOSION

55. This 1949 picture brings back memories of the sort of fog Glasgow experienced before the Clean Air Acts came into force.

56. This was the latest model of the Glasgow tram in 1947.

57. Bus and tram in Paisley Road West, 1953, approach a local accident black spot.
Note the skid marks !

58. The Mosspark-Pollokshields tram provides a convenient resting post for this representative of Billy Smart's Circus ! June 1954.

59. On September 1st 1962 a quarter of a million Glaswegians gathered in the streets in torrential rain to wave goodbye to the last of the 'caurs'.

60. Conductor George Ballantyne issues the last tickets on the last tram which left from Dumbarton Road, Yoker. Some Glaswegians spent the whole day travelling on the trams, going from one side of the city to the other.

61. Youngsters putting their pennies on the line for the last time as the last tram passes.

62. The procession marking the last tram was led by a horse drawn tram which left the depot at Ruby Street, but locals were outraged when they discovered the driver, Robert Skinner, and the horses, Teddy and Falcon, were on loan from the Edinburgh Co-operative Society!

63. This redundant Glasgow tram was loaded onto a ship for France where it went on display in a Paris motor museum. It was cut into two sections for the journey and here the lower deck is lowered aboard a cargo ship at the docks.

64. The scene in Edinburgh Road in October 1973 as bus crews refused to take school children home. The one man bus crews said they could not handle the bus and deal with vandalism and unruly behaviour. More than 4,000 pupils of Cranhill, St Gregory's and St Andrews were affected. Most of the children lived in Easterhouses or Barlanark and had to walk home until the dispute was resolved.

65. Hogmanay 1987 and it's freewheeling time as no charge buses are laid on for early morning revellers.

6. It never came into use on scheduled services but here was a £70,000 'Bendibus' on test in Glasgow in the 1970s.

67. A 22-man team was put onto renovating the paddle steamer *Waverley* at Anderston Quay, courtesy of the Jobs Creation Scheme.

68. The *Waverley* has had a chequered career. In 1993 freak tides lifted the paddle steamer from her berthing and grounded her on the way down.

69. Things have also been very up and down for the sailing ship *Carrick*, the last surviving wool clipper in the world. In March 1992 she eventually made her last trip down the Clyde after sinking at her moorings several times. Here she squeezes underneath Jamaica Bridge with just a few feet to spare.

71. Happier times. The *Carrick* moves to moorings at Customs House Quay in March 1954. The Firemaster had decreed that her berth at Glasgow bridge was unsafe.

70. In January 1978 the ship, used as a club by the RNVR, grounded on the bottom at Customs House Quay on an exceptionally low tide - and stuck fast.

75. It was reported in 1966 that "entering the control tower at Abbotsinch is like walking into Dr Who's police box". This was the white heat of technology in those days as Abbotsinch opened for business.

72. *Above* Old Renfrew Airport in 1952.

73. This was the interior of the new Renfrew Airport building in November 1954. It was regarded as the last word in design and architecture - achieved at the cost of £260,000 which was a stupendous sum in those days.

74. The exterior of the main airport building take shape, April 1954.

76. The sight of an airliner was a novelty in 1950. Here people queue to look inside one at old Renfrew Airport.

77. There was controversy over the building of the main runway for the new Abbotsinch Airport as it involved the destruction of a local graveyard.

78. This caused a stir in 1957 when it was revealed that Scots aircraft technicians at Renfrew maintenance base were working on former Canadian Mark V Sabre jet fighters handed over to the German air force.

79. Lourdes bound pilgrims are waved off at Central Station in 1955 well before the days of mass air travel.

80. *Left* June 1987 and Glasgow Airport celebrates its 21st anniversary with a cake.

81. Inside the signal box at Central Station.

82. Completion of the £11.5m. Kingston Bridge in 1970. Concrete labourer Pat McAuley finishes the job.

83. In November 1970, in the first icy grip of winter, dozens of cars went out of control on the new Kingston Bridge. Power to the heating system designed to keep the bridge ice free had not been turned on because of a wrangle between the electricity board and the Corporation !

84. Scaffolders at work in the Clyde Tunnel, 1963, as it nears completion.

5. The Queen opens the Clyde Tunnel, 1963.

86. Maintaining air ventilators in the tunnel, 1963.

87. Unconventional transport. The Unionist candidate for Woodside, W G Bennett, supplied a pony and trap to take voters to the polls in October 1951. Miss Gillian Richardson and Miss May Deans are on their way to cast their vote. Looks like they'll be voting for Bennett.

88. Terror arrives on the streets of Glasgow. The first traffic wardens gather in 1967 in the cover of a lane off Bothwell Street.

ALL IN A DAY'S WORK

89. A classic image of the Clyde, June 1971, as John Brown's went into liquidation.

90. Good times for the Clyde. Workers at John Brown's Shipyard, who have built the *Rangitane*, pose for a photograph before the launch, June 1949.

91. Launch of the *Rangitane*, 1949.

2. The shop steward - hated by the bosses, loved by the workers. Alex Jamieson of Fairfields.

3. This 'superloo' was installed by Scott's of Greenock in 1966. It was regarded as remarkable at the time !

4 Shop stewards from Fairfields No 1 study work techniques, 1966.

5. The times a changing. New attitudes at Fairfields.

6. Richard Dimbleby, the Panorama presenter, surveys the Fairfields yard.

97. The *Empress of Britain* takes shape at Fairfields in 1955.

98. Down the John Brown's slipway for the *Transvaal Castle* in January 1961.

99. Clyde built. A classic picture of a pneumatic rivetter at work in 1945.

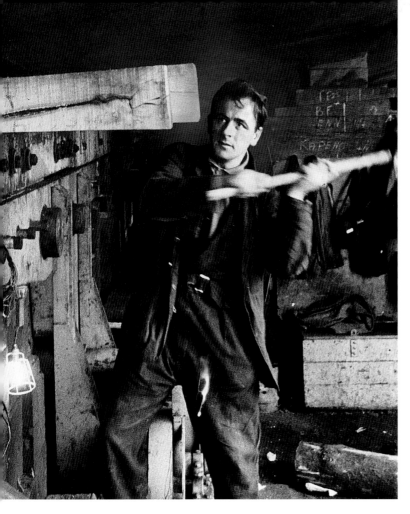

100. Worker Andrew Wilson prepares the Q E 2 for her launch.

101. *Top right* The designers and architects who created the Q.4 (later to be known as the Q E 2) gather at John Brown's.

102. H M The Queen launched the proud liner.

103. Workers on the Q E 2 prepare to cross the Atlantic, after the first launch, to complete work en route to New York.

104. September 20 1967 and one of the proudest days in the history of the Clyde as the Q E 2 is launched. Crowds pour down to the river.

105. The Q E 2 is nudged out into the river.

109. The picture that says it all. Stagers Thomas Grattan, John Speirs and Ian Knox working on Hull 248.

06. John Brown's goes into liquidation and the UCS work-in led by shop steward Jimmy Reid fights to save jobs in shipbuilding. Marathon took over in April 1972 and the workers then cheered the development.

07. Young apprentices from Brown's march in Glasgow, August 1971.

08. Even small children were on the 60,000 strong march. Three-year-old Joanne Russell from Clydebank.

110. *Left* The face of the yards. Ninety-year-old William Clary of Port Glasgow worked 56 years with Scott Lithgows as a shipwright.

111. Tough times. Empty stocks and closed gates at the Harland & Wolff yard in Govan, 1964.

112. Mass meeting of striking workers at Singer's in Clydebank, March 1951.

113. The finalists in the Miss Imp Overalls Contest at the Rootes factory in Linwood, 1963.

114. The 100th birthday of Barr's Irn Bru, September 1987. These kids from schools in the east end were invited to the celebrations for the drink made from girders.

NO BUSINESS LIKE
SHOW BUSINESS

115. Elvis Presley, with Mrs Georgina Lehar, at Glasgow's Prestwick Airport, 1960. This was the only time the King touched British soil. It is recorded he looked around and uttered three immortal words, "Where am I ?"

116. Sir Harry Lauder, the miner's son who became a favourite of King George V, was a comedian and singer with an international reputation pictured here at the Kelvin Hall in 1957.

117. Cliff Richards decked out in tartan by STV for the programme *Cliff in Scotland*.

118. Long time favourite Andy Stewart photographed in 1969.

19. Tommy Steele has his arm in a sling on his visit to Glasgow in 1959.

20. *Above right* Larry Marshall was an enormously popular entertainer, especially for his 60s STV programme *The One O'Clock Gang*.

21. Singer Ronnie Carroll was 'captured' by Glasgow Students Charity Queen Elisabeth Hoyle in the 60s. Here he is being held in her flat in Hyndland. Reo Stakis paid £100 for his release.

22. Rikki Fulton and Larry Marshall, 1969.

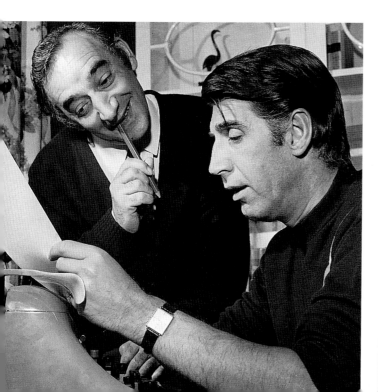

123. Pantomime. *Cinderella* to be precise. Skiffle star Lonnie Donegan attacks the ivories with Stanley Baxter and Ronnie Corbett looking on. December 1966.

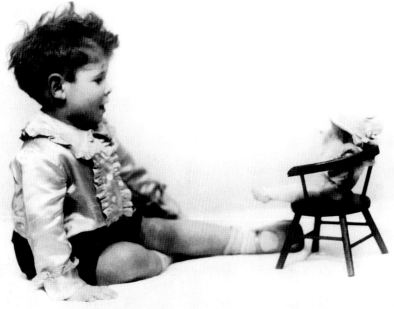

124. A rather younger Stanley Baxter - at two and-a-half-years old. He remains a firm favourite in Glasgow where audiences pack the house for his pantomimes and readers snap up his *Parliamo Glasgow* books.

125. Hot pants and thigh boots for pop singer Lulu arriving at Glasgow Airport,
February 1971.

126. Lulu, aged five.

27. *Top left* Glasgow TV personality, model and compere Carol Smillie as a big girl when she took up *The Wheel of Fortune* job.

28. Who would have guessed? Carol as a rather smaller girl.

29. May 1968 and a young Cilla Black visits her cousin Jimmy Cullen and his family at their Drumchapel home.

30. Good to be home! Sheena Easton back in Glasgow in October 1980 for a concert at the Theatre Royal.

131. TV crimebusters. *Extreme left* Robbie Coltrane, acclaimed for his portrayal of a dippy, dipsomaniac shrink in *Cracker*, opens a new art shop in Queen Street, with the help 7 year-old Joni Kilmurry.

132. On location. Actor Mark McManus, world famous for his portrayal of tough Glasgow cop, DCI Taggart.

133. *Left, below* Mark Mcmanus at Hyndland Secondary to give out prizes in a crime prevention competiton. December 1986.

134. Another successful series was BBC TV's *Rab C Nesbitt*. Here the Nesbitts are apparently about to depart for Spain and, no doubt, wreak mayhem there.

135. Also set in Glasgow was the hilarious *City Lights* in which Gerard Kelly played the role of hapless would-be writer Willie Melvin.

136. Lex Maclean was the star of the summer show at the Pavilion in 1965.

137. It's hard to know which was the greatest attraction at the Kelvin Hall motor show in 1971: Jackie Stewart, model Julie Hamilton or the punchy Cortina 2000 GT.

DEDICATED FOLLOWERS
OF FASHION

138. Queen's Park Dance in Glasgow, December 1957. The smooth looking Mr Omand seems to have his leg in plaster so presumably he didn't get much of the jigging in. Nevertheless, he seems to have some well dressed admirers . . .

139. A ball gown on display at Copland and Lye's department store in the fifties.

140. Male fashion of the day is demonstrated by John Park, President of the SFA, as he arrives for work, January 1958.

141. Fashion of the fifties.

42. Seventeen-year-old Heather Scott was a synthetic swinger in 1970. Her entire outfit was made from synthetic materials: skirt in Acrilan, blouse from Tricel, PVC boots, polyurethane coat and scarf from knitted Orlon. Lovely.

43. *Above right* In December 1969 it was reckoned this was the style for the 70s - the peasant girl look. Unfortunately, the 70s turned out to be nothing like as stylish . . .

44. This outfit turned every head in Glasgow in the winter of 1970.

145. 1969 saw Glasgow's first Hippy Wedding. The groom was dressed in jeans and the bride wore a black coat, which cost 6d. at a jumble sale, over a multi-coloured dress. They went off on honeymoon to Loch Lomond "for an Easter rave-up". Shock horror.

147. Flower power in Glasgow's George Square, September 1967. When the flower children kissed - and picked the flowers - the plods moved in.

146. Glasgow rocker with a slash on his face is led away by the law, April 1980.

148. For several years the most notorious motorcycle gang was the Blue Angels. The Glasgow chapter was founded in 1963 and these representatives are pictured after their court appearance following the 10th birthday party.

9. This more up to date biker gear from 1989 is certainly sartorially more attractive. Linda Mackay Brown from Bellshill modelled the latest in leather gear for the UK Festival of Wheels Exhibition at the SECC in Glasgow.

SALE SHIRT 25!

SALE TROUSER SUIT £4!

150. This 1970 outfit cost all of £10.

151. *Right* Late sixties styles on show in Glasgow. Left to right: Marilyn Docherty, Moira Macrae, Fiona MacGregor, Andrea McIntyre, Joy Redfern.

152. A couple of, er, unusual creations from Glasgow School of Art's 21st Annual Fashion Show, May 1973.

153. Crowds gather for the lates summer fashions in Argyle Street, May 1992.

154 & 5 Tartan is the only true hardy perennial whether worn by man - in the shape of Douglas Milne of Queen Street's Muji store - or woman - in the more shapely form of the model on the left.

SHOPPING

156. In May 1947, Mrs Cullen of Glenturret Street and Mrs Ferguson of Eglinton Street were first in line at 6 a.m. for the 'once-a-month' sale of clothing at half ration coupon rate.

157. The Sale queue outside Arnott-Simpson's Jamaica Street Store in September 1953.

158. The queue was almost 400 yards long for the sale in Milletts store in Union Street in August 1958.
Apparently, there were shirts at 1s 11d (10p.), corduroy trousers at 12s 6d and golf jackets at 7s 11d.
The shop was selling off £6,000 worth of fire damaged stock, hence the amazing bargains.

159. The traditonal Glasgow 'steamie' of the 1940

160. A 'modern' steamie opened at Osborne Street Saltmarket, in 1955. It was then described as the answer to a housewife's prayer with 'drying tumblers operating on the hot-air principle'. It was popular with local housewives who could do a day's washing in an hour.

161. This new launderette, with ten auto-washers and tumble dryers, opened in Anderston in 1976. It replaced Cranstonhill Baths, a traditional steamie where the wash would take five or six hours. A patron recalled, "You wore wellie boots and a waterproof apron. The drying facilities were very bad so you would need a pram to carry the washing home. . . washdays in place like this are bliss."

Housewives dream.

GD 8259

A DAILY RECORD Photograph

52. Amazement at this 1955 piece of state-of-the-art technonlogy.

163. Nevertheless. some women preferred the traditonal wash houses and there were demonstrations in 1971 urging their retention.

164. Mary Quant - often credited with the invention of the mini-skirt - arrives at Renfrew Airport in 1963 where she is met by businessman Hugh Fraser, whose father operated a retail empire.

165. Sir Hugh Fraser - as he became - had a mixed business and personal career. Pictured with cigarette and ashtray - he was a 40 a day man - he would ultimately die of lung cancer.

166. The opening of a Sir Hugh store in Sauchiehall Street. Sir Hugh Fraser is pictured with Janis Sue Smith, daughter Patricia Fraser, Marlene Goldie and Shona Kennedy. The venture was not a success.

67. The Barras have long been a feature of the landscape of Glasgow. The appearance changed somewhat in 1954 when part of the market acquired a roof. Here construction is going on in Kent Street.

68. Christmas rush at The Barras for stallholder Willie Kane, December 1973.

169. Legendary Leon Bernard, the herbalist, pictured in 1951.

170. Bang up to date.
Barras babes at the
Barras Fashion Show,
June 1995.

THIS SPORTING LIFE

171. Rangers v. Elgin City match is kicked off by the Glasgow Charities Queen at Ibrox in January 1949.

172. Willie Waddell (1946)

173. Tommy Docherty (1957)

174. Dixie Deans

175. Old Firm game, May 1980. Roy Aitken grimaces as Gregor Stevens heads the ball.

176. Billy McNeill.

177. Tommy Forsyth (1973)

178. Andy Roxburgh

179. Triumphant Alex Rae, captain of Partick Thistle, with the League Cup,
October 1971.

180. Jock Stein with the European Cup won in Lisbon in 1967.

181. Jock Stein had a reputation for speaking his mind. Here he gives a scarf-waving supporter a tongue lashing for running onto the pitch during a game in 1977.

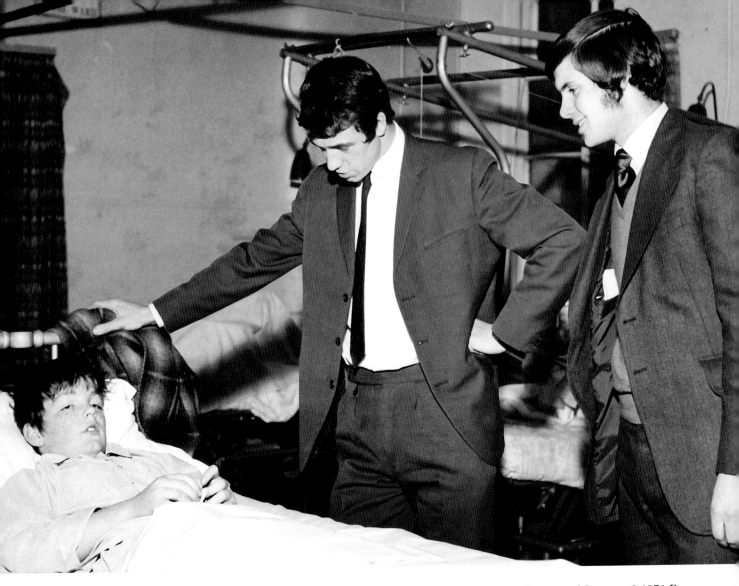

182. In the aftermath of the Ibrox disaster of January 2 1971 Rangers players visit injured fans in hospital. Dave Smith and Derek Johnstone talk to young Jim Millar of Denny in the Victoria Infirmary.

183. Shocked young fans outside the ground. Robert Mitchell, pictured here, lost his shoe in the crush.

184. *Opposite* Sixty-six fans died on unlucky Staircase 13. Here officials examine the steps. The disaster occurred in the closing minutes of the traditonal New Year derby match. Two goals in the final 60 seconds caused chaos as excited fans exiting the game tried to turn back.

185. Charge of the not so light brigade. Rangers v Celtic, May 1980.

186. Scottish Cup Final riot at Hampden, 1980.

187. A greyhound up for auction at the White City stadium. May 1972.

188. At Shawfield greyhound track and football pitch groundsmen lay sand on the waterlogged surface. January 1959.

89. *Opposite* The Great Scottish Run of 1994. Marathon runners enter West George Street.

90. Liz McColgan wins the 1500 metres at the Kelvin Hall, January 1989.

91. Dunky Wright heads marathon runners carrying fiery crosses at the completion of the Edinburgh - Glasgow Marathon Race in May 1949. Here the runners arrive at Ibrox Stadium.

192. Jim Watt wins at Kelvin Hall against Sean O'Grady. November 1980.

HOLD THE FRONT PAGE

193. The gales of January 1968 wrought enormous damage in Glasgow. Here 83-year-old invalid
Frank Hopper, dressed up for the occasion, leaves his Charing Cross home by turntable ladder.
Across the landing, a neighbour had died when a chimney stack crashed through the roof.

94. *Left* Two young victims of the gales.

95. *Above* In a crowded room at Foresthall Hospital victims of the gales were gathered together pondering an uncertain future.

96. The gable end of this tenement was completely torn away.

97. More than two months after the gales some people were still living with the after effects. Jessie Cooper and her daughter in their kitchen where basins caught the water still pouring in. March 1968.

198. Gale damage at Govanhill Street. The end of the tenement is torn away and these men try to salvage a radiogram from the wreckage.

199. This might look like the Arctic but it was the Clyde at Pointhouse in January 1945. Clyde traffic was disrupted by floating ice and small craft were lifted out of the water.

200. When a storage plant in the East end of Glasgow was flooded in September 1985, 14,000 empty barrels were swept into the Clyde. Here they are near the suspension bridge at Dixon Street. Some were spotted as far down river as Dumbarton Rock.

201. The James Watt Street fire. Twenty-two workers died behind the barred windows of the upholstery warehouse where they worked. November 1968.

202. Clarkston disaster. Twenty shoppers were killed and more than 100 injured when a faulty gas main ignited at the shopping centre at Clarkston Toll. October 1971.

203. The Grosvenor Hotel was destroyed by fire during the firemens' strike of January 1978. Here owner Reo Stakis is seen outside the smouldering shell the next morning. The hotel was demolished and rebuilt in the same style.

4. The Kilbirnie Street warehouse fire. Seven firemen died in the August 1972 blaze.

205. The line-up at the 1967 Charities Queen contest in Glasgow. Fashions are still demure in Glasgow. The Swinging Sixties took a little longer to arrive in Glasgow . . .

206. By 1973 fashions at the contest were less demure. As the *Record* put it "sixteen pretty maids in a row with three things in common - good looks, brains and the burning ambition to win." All quite politically uncorrect today, of course. But nice.

207. Students' flour battle in Pitt Street, 1970. Some students were arrested.

98. The 1988 Glasgow Garden Festival was an enormous popular success. This was the Coca Cola roller ride. Pictured here is 84 year-old David Grindlay from Dumbarton getting his birthday thrill.

209. A young Jimmy Boyle leaves court with his girlfiend in March 1965 having been found Not Proven on an assault charge.

210. Boyle married Sarah Trevelyan while serving a 15 year sentence in Barlinnie's Special Unit for murder. His wife was a visiting psychiatrist.

211. Right Paddy Meehan claimed he was framed by MI5. He had been convicted of murder, served seven years of a life sentence and been released on a Royal Pardon. He published a book on his experiences in 1989 but, somewhat defamatory, had to sell the volume in the streets after booksellers refused to handle it.

212. *Extreme left* 'Gentle' Johnny Ramensky, master safe blower and prison escapee after a release celebration at his Eglinton Street home. In the war he was released from prison to go behind enemy lines, crack safes and steal German war secrets.

213. *Left* Murderer and psychopath Peter Manuel. He was convicted and exceuted in 1958 after a string of murders involving young girls and the members of two families.

214. Easterhouse folk take advantage of a 1968 weapons amnesty designed to take anti-social implements out of the hands of the gangs.

215. Demolition of Hutcheson E flats.

216. The 24-floor tower block at Roystonhill is blown up. In 1992 it was the biggest-ever flat block to be demolished in Britain.

217. Blowdown !

218. Glasgow's Miles Better ! Lord Provost Michael Kelly brought in the successful slogan and the campaign to rehabilitate the city's image. But it was such a tiring job !